This book belongs to:

_____

MY LIGHT SHINES THROUGH

Your light must shine before people in such a way that they may see your good works.
Matthew 5:16

I ENCOURAGE OTHERS

So encourage each other and build each other up, just as you are already doing.
1 Thessalonians 5:11

I GUARD MY HEART

Above all else, guard your heart, for everything you do flows from it. Proverbs 4:23

THE LORD IS MY LIGHT

The Lord is my light
and my salvation;
whom shall I fear?

Psalm 27:1

I AM VALUABLE

The very hairs on your head are all numbered. So don't be afraid; you are more valuable to God than a whole flock of sparrows. Luke 12:7

BE KIND AND COMPASSIONATE

Be kind and loving to each other.
Forgive each other the same as God
forgave you through Christ Jesus.
Ephesians 4:32

MY LIFE IS FILLED WITH GOOD THINGS

Taste and see that the Lord is good. Psalm 34:8

Come to me, all you who are
weary and burdened, and I will
give you rest.
Matthew 11:28

Made in the USA
Monee, IL
06 April 2025

15264010R00059